Contents

ap·ro·pos

The Two Realms and the Separation of Church and State

Joel Biermann

CONCORDIA PUBLISHING HOUSE · SAINT LOUIS

Published by Concordia Publishing House
3558 S. Jefferson Ave., St. Louis, MO 63118-3968
1-800-325-3040 • cph.org

1 2 3 4 5 6 7 8 9 10 34 33 32 31 30 29 28 27 26 25

Introduction

Each peculiar stream within the great flow of the one Christian faith has at least one or two distinctive teachings or practices particularly identified with that tradition. Calvinism keys on the sovereignty of God and the TULIP markers, Rome centers on ecclesiastical authority and clerical hierarchy culminating in the pope, the Orthodox prize the fathers and liturgical form, and Baptists emphasize the necessity of human freedom and choice. For Lutheranism, the centrality of justification and the distinction between Law and Gospel are typically favorable identifiers within the wider Christian community. Less enthusiastically applauded, but just as distinctively Lutheran, is the distinction between the two kingdoms or realms, which is often treated as a characteristically Lutheran idea. Yet while the terminology and concept may be familiar enough, and while many Christians and most Lutherans will claim an adequate grasp of the basic content of the doctrine of the two kingdoms, an accurate understanding of the actual teaching is far from common, even among those who bear the reformer's name. Part of the problem may be the widespread acceptance of grossly oversimplified and inaccurate presentations of the teaching and a consequent overconfidence in one's mastery of the material. In truth, what is offered as a summary of the teaching is too often not only inaccurate but disastrous. Never was this more tragically evident than in Germany before and during the Second World War.

Raising the Nazi specter in the first paragraph of an introduction may well seem gratuitously overdramatic—and maybe it is;

still, I believe invoking this grim failure of Christian confession is warranted to illustrate the profound significance of holding doctrinal ideas either faithfully or errantly and acting accordingly. This is true specifically with the two realms but also applies more broadly to all doctrinal endeavor. When it comes to doctrine, a great deal is always at stake not only for this temporal life but also certainly, and very often frequently, for the new eternal life fully manifest at Christ's return. And although perhaps not many would rank the teaching of the two realms as a doctrine bearing the weighty significance of eternal salvation hanging in the balance, there is no doubt that a mishandling of the teaching absolutely can result in what amounts to a hell on earth.

It was theological reflection on the horror of the Second World War and the appalling complicity with the Third Reich, which came far too easily for far too many Christians in Germany, that led to the notoriety or perhaps more accurately infamy of what was then christened as the "Lutheran doctrine of the two kingdoms." As Robert Benne notes, the label was not intended to be positive.[1] The veracity of the charge that the "two kingdoms doctrine" was the root of the problem behind the failure of the *Deutsche Christen* will be considered in chapter 3; for now, it is the term itself that is of interest. Before the twentieth century, the Lutheran teaching on the two realms had not been singled out as necessarily in need of a particular name or label; it was simply part of the church's teaching as outlined by Philip Melanchthon in his succinct presentation of the Reformation's core teaching that comprises the first twenty-one articles of the Augsburg Confession.

---

1 Robert Benne, *The Paradoxical Vision: A Public Theology for the Twenty-First Century* (Fortress Press, 1995), 78–79.

The Augsburg Confession

The first part of the Augsburg Confession follows a smooth narrative arc, recounting the work of God creating the world and then redeeming and preserving it through the mission of Christ and the Spirit-driven activity of His church and finally, at last, fully restoring and glorifying that world at Christ's return. After emphasizing the work of the church through its proclamation of the Gospel and its faithful practice of the Sacraments, in Article 16, Melanchthon confesses the propriety of Christian participation in the temporal realm, or the things pertaining to life in this world. The contents of this article were likely highlighted in an intentional effort to create as much space as possible between the Lutheran reformers and the errant ideas of more radical teachers of the day who were often dismissive of or even hostile toward the material world and its necessary structures. Yet Melanchthon is not exclusively polemic in his presentation, and even without the catalyst of theological error that needed to be called out and condemned, the faithful teaching contained in Article 16 belonged in the church's confession. In his written confession of the Lutheran faith, Melanchthon was bound to affirm the goodness of the created world and its activities and does so at precisely the right place in the story—toward the end of his twenty-one-article, summary confession of the church's correct teaching. In other words, any telling of the *regula fidei* (rule of faith) or the *corpus doctrinae* (body of doctrine) that from the beginning has guided and normed the Christian Church's faithful proclamation and right confession must of necessity always include some articulation of the teaching of the two realms.

In early print editions of the Augsburg Confession, the German text gave Article 16 the title "Concerning Public Order and Secular Government"; the Latin translation was at once more concise and more expansive in scope: "Civil Affairs." The article itself confirms the accuracy of both titles as it begins with an affirmation of God's role in government but then goes on to indicate that there is more to the affairs of civil life than merely governmental rule and the corresponding obedience of Christian citizens:

> Concerning public order and secular government it is taught that all political authority, orderly government, laws, and good order in the world are created and instituted by God and that Christians may without sin exercise political authority; be princes and judges; pass sentences and administer justice according to imperial and other existing laws; punish evildoers with the sword; wage just wars; serve as soldiers; buy and sell; take required oaths; possess property; be married; etc.
>
> Condemned here are the Anabaptists who teach that none of the things indicated above is Christian.[2]

Essentially, everything that was denied and shunned by the Anabaptists with their propensity for wholesale disregard or dismissal of the created realm was endorsed and embraced by Melanchthon and the Lutheran confessors.

Melanchthon, though, did not exhaust his vitriol criticizing the mistaken theology of the radical reformers on one side. In the second half of Article 16 of the Augsburg Confession, he leveled a stern rebuke also against the misguided ideas of the Roman Catholic opponents on the other side:

> Also condemned are those who teach that Christian perfection means physically leaving house and home, spouse

2 AC XVI 1–3, German. The Anabaptist refusal to condone secular civil authority of any Christian participation in such political ruling stemmed from their conviction that Jesus' command not to take the sword was unequivocal and fully applicable to all areas of life, including that of government.

> and child, and refraining from the above-mentioned activities. In fact, the only true perfection is true fear of God and true faith in God. For the gospel teaches an internal, eternal reality and righteousness of the heart, not an external, temporal one. The gospel does not overthrow secular government, public order, and marriage but instead intends that a person keep all this as a true order of God and demonstrate in these walks of life Christian love and true good works according to each person's calling. Christians, therefore, are obliged to be subject to political authority and to obey its commands and laws in all that may be done without sin. But if a command of the political authority cannot be followed without sin, one must obey God rather than any human beings (Acts 5[:29]).[3]

Article 16 makes clear that, with its monastic obsession, Rome was undercutting the right functioning of the temporal realm and utterly destroying the goodness and beauty of ordinary life with its mundane vocations tied to house, home, and secular occupations. Melanchthon, it is evident, had more on his mind than just politics and government; the scope of his concern in Article 16 ranged out into every corner of regular life in this world. The significance of this emphasis on Christian life fully invested in the realities of the temporal world is critical and will be given appropriate attention in the first chapter. For now, it is important to recognize that the duality of God's two realms should never be thought of as synonymous with concerns related only to issues of church and state.

There is, admittedly, good reason for discussions about God's two realms to narrow down to a restricted focus on the often tense and sometimes conflicted relationship between ecclesial and

---

3 AC XVI 4–7, German.

political authority. These questions are of keen interest, no doubt, simply because so much is at stake in the give and take between church and state. Questions about the interactions between these two authorities are also interesting as power and control at work in these interactions, whether regnant or ascendent, has shifted back and forth significantly through the centuries. In the early years after the resurrection of Jesus, the church endured the indifference and then hostility of the overwhelmingly powerful Roman Empire; yet, led and fed by the Holy Spirit, the church confidently followed her Lord to breathtaking growth. The explosive impact of Christianity eventuated in the church's surprising triumph in the days of Constantine and the eventual capitulation of secular power to the hegemony of the church achieved in the late medieval world. Luther would boast that he brought this unhealthy situation of churchly domination over secular authority to an end, and in time, modernity eventually brought the tenuous but enduring and familiar rapprochement of church and state expressed in a variety of ways in Europe and the new world. H. Richard Niebuhr famously and iconically described the assorted versions of Christendom as it was manifest in America with his widely known five types or categories presented in his influential book *Christ and Culture*.[4] In the twenty-first century, church and state questions remain relevant and pressing, but they are shifting again as Christendom atrophies and evaporates along with whatever prestige and influence it once enjoyed. Now we are left with the assorted and unsteady efforts of American Christians to discover or perhaps negotiate the best way forward in a strange new world. The wisdom and success of some of the more noteworthy of these efforts to find a new way will be evaluated in chapter 3.

4 Niebuhr's five types have been variously maligned and attacked but have proven remarkably resilient and useful for thinking about the church and state experience in the United States. His five types are Christ against culture, Christ of culture, Christ above culture, Christ and culture in paradox, and Christ transforming culture. H. Richard Niebuhr, *Christ and Culture* (Harper & Row, 1951), xxxvii–lv.

It is apparent already from the confession at Augsburg that the teaching of God's two realms was about much more than a circumscribed interest in questions of church and state. And it is also evident that Melanchthon did not consider his articulation of God's reality with regard to life in the temporal world in Article 16 to be a uniquely Lutheran idea; nor did he present the teaching as a formula or paradigm worthy of its own label. Like the distinction between Law and Gospel (God's twofold message to the world), the distinction between the two realms (God's twofold way of operating in the world) simply functioned as a pervasive presupposition at work beneath the theological endeavors of Luther, Melanchthon, and their fellow reformers. The distinction between the realms was a tool to be utilized in theological work, so it did not achieve the status of being counted among the foundational theological loci (i.e., "common places" for gathering doctrinal content), nor was it elevated with a distinctive title like "doctrine of the two kingdoms." The two realms teaching was merely a taken-for-granted axiom describing God's activity in His creation through two related but very different modes of operation with their corresponding God-appointed institutions of church and state. This means that understanding the teaching of the two realms requires an appreciation for the basic theological approach and undergirding assumptions that drove all of Luther's thinking and the answers he provided to the urgent questions of his day. I will do my best to make these foundational ideas plain as the basic contours of the teaching are taken up more fully in chapter 1.

Luther and Lutheranism

Working in Lutheran theology means working in the shadow of Martin Luther. Those of us who embrace Luther's legacy recognize that we do not blindly follow a mere man, nor do we heedlessly yield to his every theological thought, argument, or system.

Yet those who are willing to bear Luther's name typically do so without regret and see his influence and continual presence as a great asset and only rarely as a liability—though those liabilities are, quite frankly, sizable enough. But in the present discussion of the two realms, the presence of Luther and his teaching will be welcomed warmly. Still, it needs to be made clear that this book is not a Luther study but a consideration of the Lutheran way of navigating the interface between the two realms. Luther's thought matters a great deal, of course, and the precedents, commitments, and ways of operating that drove Luther continue to influence Lutherans today. I am certainly eager to be numbered among those happy to have Luther's company and his steady directing hand as I go about my own theological work almost five centuries after his death. All of this is to say that I am not in the least ashamed to be a Lutheran and earnestly follow my namesake's lead into the theological task.

What follows, then, should not be construed as a Luther book much less a historical exploration of what precisely Luther himself taught about the two realms. Indeed, the confessional subscription that binds, norms, and directs me is to the Book of Concord alone, not to Martin Luther or any of his writings beyond his catechisms and Smalcald Articles, which, of course, are contained in the Book of Concord. Rather than endlessly citing Luther or carefully exploring the nuances of his many writings on the topic of the two realms, I will try to follow Luther's method and example and simply present God's truth as confessed by His faithful church in the area of the two realms and their dynamic interrelationship.

Kingdoms or Realms?

This introduction has sought to set the stage by introducing the familiar and probably even standard term "doctrine of the two kingdoms" and then considering the confessional foundation and expression for this concept found in the normative collection of texts that comprise the Book of Concord. While the second task has been sufficiently fulfilled, something important yet remains to be said about the terminology itself. The popular default designation for the idea of God's continuing twofold reign over His fallen creation is, of course, "the doctrine of the two kingdoms." As noted above, it is good to keep in mind that this label only came into popular usage as a pejorative attack against the teaching. Although Luther himself never referenced a doctrine of the two kingdoms, he definitely used the collection of important ideas that would later be given their own particular label. Nevertheless, it is true that the term that has now become common does fit Luther's use and faithfully captures the idea of two distinct areas over which a sovereign rules, thus two kingdoms.

Beyond the awkwardness of the common moniker's disparaging origin in the aftermath of the Second World War, however, a further and more substantial difficulty arises when it is recognized that the same German word, used by Luther, *Regiment*, that is translated as "kingdom" in reference to God's twofold rule over the world is often also used by Luther and others to refer to the two contending kingdoms of God and Satan. This pair of metaphysical or transcending and undergirding kingdoms absolutely does not align with Luther's twofold distinction between the temporal and spiritual kingdoms of God's reign over the earth. And when a misguided correspondence that seeks to connect God with the spiritual kingdom and Satan with the temporal kingdom is attempted or assumed, confusion and dangerous false teaching inevitably and quickly result. This is the compelling reason for choosing a synonym other than *kingdom* to translate *Regiment*. It also explains my preferred use of the word *realm* rather than *kingdom* when discussing the twofold way that God is at work to rule and guide His creation in both the temporal and the spiritual domains. Other synonyms could also be suggested, of course, including sphere, jurisdiction, sovereignty, or domain. But among a number of Lutheran writers aware of the potential confusion over terms, *realm* has become the usual choice. Going forward, then, references to two kingdoms should be understood as referring to the two warring kingdoms of God and Satan and not the mutually compatible realms of the temporal and the spiritual; on the other hand, when the idea of God's twofold sovereignty and guidance over His fallen creation is in mind—as will be the case virtually throughout this book—then the term *realm* will be used. Again, this is not to suggest that there is an inherent problem with the term *kingdom* or a preference for *realm*; it is simply a matter of seeking clarity in the use of terminology.

Finally, one last observation needs to be made and fully appreciated before embarking on a presentation of the actual distinction between the two realms. In the twenty-first-century world of the academic community, every topic is deconstructed, atomized, examined, and eventually explained with a theory or what is purported to be a definitive description of some sort. Since few if any steps in that process are capable of true objectivity, competing and often contradictory descriptions and theories flourish, especially in the realm of the soft sciences that suffer from even fewer opportunities for a modicum of objectivity. So it is that when the practitioners of the social sciences try to explain or account for any and all forms of human behavior, whether individual or collective, theories abound. And so it is that in discussions about Luther's teaching, references will often be made to "Luther's political theory" or the "political philosophy of Lutheranism." Using this verbiage, much less entertaining the very idea that one can postulate a "political theory of Luther," can only be deemed as hopelessly and ignorantly anachronistic. Simply put, Luther did not have a political theory. In other words, Luther did not take a look around at his late medieval world of politics with its patchwork of competing feudal fiefdoms, conniving and interfering ecclesiastical lords, economic and military power games, and monarchial and aristocratic intrigue in the chaotic remnants of a phony Roman Empire and then devise a theory to explain how it all hung together.

Luther's teaching about the two realms did not arise through his careful study and reflection on what he saw going on around him, nor did he simply reprise and repackage the thought of great thinkers whom he admired. Not even Augustine's political writing can be neatly mapped to Luther's thought. In spite of what seems an obvious similarity between Augustine's two cities and Luther's two realms, the two theologians meant very different things with their respective terms. Luther was not a political theorist, and his teaching on the two realms should not be categorized as just one more theory—and a very old, outdated, and mostly irrelevant one at that. To grasp Luther's contribution and the importance of his political ideas, it is critical to recognize that Luther was not trying to explain what he saw, advance an agenda, or reconcile competing claims to authority. He was not driven by what made sense, won intellectual affirmations and friends, or offered a pragmatic reward.

Luther's ideas about God's twofold rule must be recognized as an outgrowth or a mere aspect of his all-encompassing way of seeing and understanding absolutely everything though the lens of Christian theology. Luther read Scripture, learned from the church and her fathers, and completely adopted and internalized a way of understanding human existence and the entire world that was shaped and defined always and only by the *regula fidei* of the church's true and so timeless teaching—precisely the teaching that was outlined in the Augsburg Confession. Luther was not a philosopher, politician, theorist, or even pure academician. Luther was a theologian and a pastor. He sought God's truth and then taught God's truth, nothing more and nothing less. Luther did not hesitate to use the tools and contributions of the academic community along with the newly forming science and technology of his day; but he used all of these resources in the service of theology—that is to say, the right teaching of God's truth—to which every tool, idea, theory, or fact was made to submit. It is out of this context that Luther wrote about God's way of working in the world in two distinct ways, and it is within this same framework that any faithful Lutheran presentation of the two realms of God's activity must be offered. In precisely this spirit, it is time to present and explore the teaching of the two realms.

Chapter 1
Situating the Two Realms

Sometime in the last years of the second decade of the sixteenth century, Martin Luther's long and tortuous spiritual angst came to a gracious and glorious end. Desperate to find peace with God, the young Luther famously abandoned his university studies en route to life as a lawyer and abandoned himself to the project of securing spiritual perfection through the model course prescribed by the church. The project failed. The spiritual comfort and assurance he craved and sacrificed so much to attain never materialized, and his earnest effort to secure peace with God degenerated into futility. It was when Luther was distracted from his own striving for righteousness and simply doing the job he'd been given to do, preparing his lectures on Romans for his students at the University of Wittenberg, that his spiritual torment unexpectedly came to an end. Ironically, yet necessarily, peace with God did not result from his focused efforts to find and claim it; the peace he so ardently desired came as a bolt out of the blue, a gift, in the course of fulfilling his vocation for the sake of others. Through the words of Paul's letter to the Romans, the Spirit worked on the devout monk, and Luther was utterly astounded, indeed gobsmacked, when the recognition was forced upon him by the gracious work of the Holy Spirit that the "righteousness of God" was not a thing to be earned or achieved but a gift to be received. Nothing would ever be the same again.

The insight and outcome of Luther's tower experience, evangelical breakthrough, or discovery of the Gospel, as the story above has been variously labeled, remains the vital heart of Lutheran confession. The sinner's justification by grace through faith in Jesus Christ alone is arguably the most important doctrinal expression of the entire Christian faith. This essential declaration captures the truth that captured Luther: a God who finds sinners, claims them, calls them, forgives them, raises them, and fully restores them—a God who does everything for the eternal salvation of His people. Luther staked his teaching, his thinking, his life, and his eternity on the great theological truth of the Gospel. Every faithful Lutheran since has done the same.

The stunning wonder of the Gospel—that no human merits or achieves righteousness before God or gains personal dignity, worth, or identity by individual intention, sincerity, or effort but instead receives all of these things along with life itself, peace with God and with self, confidence in the face of death, and the promise of resurrected life in Christ's eternal kingdom purely as a gift of God's grace—is rightly, and wonderfully, the core of Christian confession. But it is not the whole of Christian confession. The Gospel does not swallow up the entirety of Christian doctrine or even act as doctrinal trump when thinking theologically as if everything, including God's Law, should somehow be "gospeled" and transformed into something different. The Law is not changed by the Gospel—sinners are changed by the Gospel. And the same letter of Paul to the Romans that delivered the Gospel to Luther also gave him a completely new way of understanding his life as a redeemed and transformed sinner in God's creation—a sinner who was now learning to keep and delight in the very Law that had convicted and crushed him. Being declared forgiven by the Gospel is always directly linked to the reality of a return to life lived in the present world according to the will of God, which is but a synonym for the Law.

The final sentence in the preceding paragraph makes two significant claims that both deserve some corroborating evidence. The second idea, that the Law is synonymous with the will of God, enjoys full confessional support. The Solid Declaration of the Formula of Concord is explicit: "When we speak of good works that are in accord with the law of God (for otherwise they are not good works), the word 'law' has one single meaning, namely, the unchanging will of God, according to which human beings are to conduct themselves in this life."[1] To put it another way, the Law of God is not an alien set of rules imposed on humanity after the human-wrought disaster of the fall. Rather, the Law is simply the description of the way that God intended His entire creation to work—including the human parts of His creation. What God made perfect, man in his willful sin corrupted and destroyed, and God in His inexplicable grace then reclaimed and restored through the life, death, and resurrection of Jesus Christ. So, the Law both predates man in his fallen state and continues to norm and guide him in his redeemed state as a new creature.

This neatly brings us to the first poignant point made in that overloaded final sentence two paragraph's previous, a point elegantly affirmed by Luther in his Great Galatians Commentary of 1535:

> When I have this righteousness within me [the passive righteousness of the Gospel], I descend from heaven like the rain that makes the earth fertile. That is, I come forth into another kingdom, and I perform good works whenever the opportunity arises. If I am a minister of the Word, I preach, I comfort the saddened, I administer the sacraments. If I am a father, I rule my household and family, I train my children in piety and honesty. If I am a magistrate, I perform the office which I have received by divine command. If I am a servant, I faithfully tend to my master's affairs. In short, whoever knows for sure that

1 FC SD VI 15.

> Christ is his righteousness not only cheerfully and gladly works in his calling but also submits himself for the sake of love to magistrates, also to their wicked laws, and to everything else in this present life—even, if need be, to burden and danger. For he knows that God wants this and that this obedience pleases Him.[2]

This splendid little penultimate paragraph from Luther's introduction to his lectures on Galatians not only clinches the claim made above that the Gospel sends us back into the world to do good works, but it also captures and conveys a host of other critical concepts necessary for a faithful understanding and practice of all right theology and in particular the two realms. Indeed, this single paragraph can serve as a remarkably effective springboard to discuss precisely the driving ideas, categories, and assumptions that were at work in Luther's theology and that were especially significant for his thinking and teaching about the temporal realm and the spiritual realm. With that in mind, it will be altogether fruitful to linger on this passage, and it should be further borne in mind that this snippet from Luther is far from a one-off comment but is faithfully representative of his quite consistent theological thought on these matters.

Notice in Luther's compelling imagery about the rain falling from one kingdom (as noted in the Introduction, I'd prefer the translation *realm*) the tight relationship between what has been delivered as a gift from heaven—that is, in the individual's relationship with God, which is purely passive and grounded fully and wonderfully in God's Gospel of grace—and the life of that same individual lived in another kingdom—that is, the individual's relationships and responsibilities in the present life. This vividly illustrates the irresistible bond between realities in the spiritual

2 AE 26:11–12. Brackets added by author.

realm and the temporal realm. So, while this paragraph explicitly illustrates the two kinds of human righteousness (one passively received before God and the other actively achieved in the world), it also highlights the two realms. It is apparent from this paragraph that the two paradigms or dualities of two kinds of righteousness and two realms certainly overlap with one another, but it is also important to remember that the two kinds of righteousness and the two realms are not synonymous as each duality seeks to answer a different question. Two kinds of righteousness aims at what it means to be fully human in right relationships, and two realms clarifies how God works in His creation in a twofold way.

The two realms aspect at work in this paragraph is further highlighted when Luther begins his seemingly random list of illustrations of humans making the earth fertile through their good works in the earthly realm. Of course, the list is far from arbitrary or serendipitous. Indeed, moving from pastor to father to prince, Luther has deliberately touched on each of three medieval estates that circumscribed all of life for all people: church, home, government. Tacking on the servant at the end of the list effectively fills any potential gaps in application as those in the role of servant abounded in Luther's day essentially in all three estates.[3] By intentionally choosing the responsible office-bearer, or one who was held accountable for the right conduct and success of each realm—pastor, father, and prince—as his examples, Luther has reinforced the importance of the work that is done in every vocation in each of the three estates. One is not more holy or godly or God-pleasing than another; even the "minister of the Word" is simply doing his work in the world for the sake of those around him—just like a father and just like a prince.

---

3 One can also see the addition of the servant as Luther anticipating the move that would become common in the twentieth century when work or labor was split out from the home or household and labeled as the fourth estate or mandate in which human vocations took shape.

Luther's emphasis in this passage on these three offices, each responsible for directing the work of one of the three estates, captures another essential component of a right understanding of the two realms: those who are given the authority of leadership in each realm are established in their office by the direct action of God Himself. As Luther puts it, "If I am a magistrate, I perform the office which I have received by divine command."[4] Magistrates, or government officials, act authoritatively only because God has authorized them so to act. Since it runs counter to virtually every assumption and idea at work in our modern world, the significance of this concept deserves some deliberate and unhurried reflection to encourage careful digestion. In modernity, social structures and the authority arrangements within them are thought to spring from a myriad host of complicated cultural, physiological, and psychological factors—none of which, naturally, is the omniscient, omnipotent, benevolent will of God. In the modern world, it is a foregone conclusion that authority arises from within the context of the world—from evolutionary developments or social contracts or brute brandishing of power. In line with faithful Christian confession, however, Luther and his trustworthy heirs hold to the conviction that all authority derives from God Himself, who wills and directs all of it as He pleases.

This is precisely the point Luther makes in his Large Catechism explanation of the Fourth Commandment: "Thus all who are called masters stand in the place of parents and must derive from them their power and authority to govern. They are all called fathers in the Scriptures because in their sphere of authority they have been commissioned as fathers and ought to have fatherly hearts toward their people."[5] God established the authority structures of this world when He established the order and design of

4 AE 26:12.

5 LC I 142.

this world. Adam and Eve were tasked with exercising dominion or authority over the creation. The authority of government and of the church both extend from that initial authority. As Luther summarizes in the Large Catechism, "So we have introduced three kinds of fathers in this commandment: fathers by blood, fathers of a household, and fathers of the nation. In addition, there are also spiritual fathers."[6] Each father in each estate functions for the sake of the creation. So, it is that each of the authoritative positions of responsibility and leadership in church, home, and state amounts to an office (or *Amt* in German). No one can act in one of these areas without the appropriate authorization to do so, and that authority comes from God Himself as it is disseminated through the structures and ways of operating that He has established and allowed in His providential ordering of the world. While in modern democratic society the idea of authority vested in an office by God's decree and action may be held to be of no account or a mere vestige of a mercifully bygone era, in Lutheran thought, the idea of authority grounded in God's design carries a great deal of weight, and appreciation of this truth is essential if the teaching of the two realms is to be rightly understood.

That same paragraph from Luther's Galatians commentary, now cited several paragraphs ago, holds two more significant lessons that will help establish a solid foundation for rightly understanding the teaching of the two realms. Notably, Luther embraces the idea of vocations: "Whoever knows for sure that Christ is his righteousness . . . cheerfully and gladly works in his calling."[7] Doing whatever vocation God has given a person to do is that individual's way of living faithfully within the world, or within the temporal realm of this created life. God arranges His creation and His human creatures within it to work together to accomplish His plan

---

6 LC I 158.

7 AE 26:12.

for the creation. Each human does this work by doing the vocation, or more accurately, vocations, that he or she has been given to do. The second and final lesson that cannot be missed is that once the structure of human life in this world has been established within the framework of the three estates and our vocations within each, it is necessary that humans live within this design. In other words, obedience to authority is essential: "Whoever knows for sure that Christ is his righteousness . . . submits himself for the sake of love to magistrates, also to their wicked laws, and to everything else in this present life—even, if need be, to burden and danger. For he knows that God wants this and that this obedience pleases Him."[8] Luther's conviction about the importance of submission to human authority as being submission to God claimed a significant and consistent place in his thinking about life in the temporal realm, and it must remain an important idea for those who claim his legacy.

Luther did not express these ideas this way merely because he happened to be a product of his time—though he certainly was thoroughly shaped by his time and place in history, of course. It is important to recognize, nevertheless, that Luther's main cues for his theological thinking about the civil realm and its government did not come from his feudal society or strict upbringing or hierarchical ecclesiastical experience. The foremost influence on Luther's thinking about the temporal realm was above all else the Bible, specifically the teaching and examples of Jesus, Peter, and Paul. Luther thought the way he did about the structures of life in this world because he read and believed the Bible. No doubt, he read within and through the context of the gestalt of his place and time, but he also read in the context of the apostolic *regula fidei*—the standard teaching of the church that had been passed

---

8 AE 26:12.

down with varying degrees of faithfulness and then confessed with precision, clarity, and beauty at Augsburg.

The church's faithful teachers and the body of doctrine, which is the church's confession, taught Luther how to read the scriptural texts. Contrary to the practice of some, Luther did not develop ideas, explanations, and systems that made sense or supported the status quo or advanced an agenda he found appealing and then set off in search of Scripture to validate his argument. Luther simply read, received, and learned what God had established and revealed about the workings of the temporal realm. Reading as he had been taught by the church also meant that Luther did not engage in a proof-text approach in his doctrinal work; in other words, his doctrinal modus operandi was not to pronounce some proposition or declaration and then prop it up with an assortment of ostensibly supporting verses that may or may not have applied. No, Luther did theology in a faithful and exemplary right way: constrained by the whole of God's revelation and in conversation with the church and her teachers that had taught him how to do, believe, think, and teach.

The narrative arc of the scriptural account of God's story culminating in the earthly ministry, death, and resurrection of God's incarnate Son, Jesus, is the revelation that guided Luther's thinking about the world around him. That story leads to an appreciation of the order, structure, and precise design that God followed from the beginning of His creative work and that God built into the creation itself. This provides the context and source for all right thinking and teaching about the two realms.

Venturing into an exegetical consideration of all the scriptural texts that provide foundation and context for the teaching of the two realms lies well beyond the scope of this deliberately slim text. To provide a representative and normative sample of the overall biblical teaching, it will be enough to call attention to a few of the most significant texts. All three of the Synoptic Gospels record the

Holy Week encounter between Jesus and those opposed to Him for both theological and political reasons and who together offered the seemingly innocent question about paying taxes to Caesar. Naturally, Jesus was the master of both the situation and the questioners and gave this brilliant and now familiar response: "Render to Caesar the things that are Caesar's, and to God the things that are God's."[9] The maxim silenced His critics and rightly amazed everyone but did not shed much light on the actual problem—it still remains to sort out exactly what belongs to whom. But the distinction between the realms implicit in Jesus' response found fuller treatment from Paul and Peter as directed by the Holy Spirit.

The apostle Paul offered what is probably the most complete and important expression of the Christian attitude toward governmental authority. This foundational text deserves quoting in full:

> Let every person be subject to the governing authorities. For there is no authority except from God, and those that exist have been instituted by God. Therefore whoever resists the authorities resists what God has appointed, and those who resist will incur judgment. For rulers are not a terror to good conduct, but to bad. Would you have no fear of the one who is in authority? Then do what is good, and you will receive his approval, for he is God's servant for your good. But if you do wrong, be afraid, for he does not bear the sword in vain. For he is the servant of God, an avenger who carries out God's wrath on the wrongdoer. Therefore one must be in subjection, not only to avoid God's wrath but also for the sake of conscience. For because of this you also pay taxes, for *the authorities* are ministers of God, attending to this very thing. Pay to

9 Mark 12:17.

all what is owed to them: taxes to whom taxes *are owed,* revenue to whom revenue is owed, respect to whom respect is owed, honor to whom honor is owed.[10]

One could easily devote an entire chapter or even book to the task of unpacking all that is going on in this single section of Romans, but for the present task, a few key observations will suffice. The fact that God Himself establishes rulers in their office is overwhelmingly driven home by this text—though remarkably, there are those driven by divergent doctrinal commitments who perform incredible feats of exegetical gymnastics and malpractice to insist that because it bears the sword government can only be considered as utterly antithetical to genuine Christian confession.[11] For good or ill, however, governments and their rulers are God's servants. It should not be missed that Paul explicitly declares this truth three times in these seven verses using a pair of potent Greek words to make his point. The word translated "servant" in verse 4 is *diakonia*, and "ministers" in verse 6 is *leitourgoi*. The former is the familiar word that makes its way into English as a particular calling in the church, and the latter is a term used in the early church to refer to priests and in the New Testament to refer to Paul, angels, and Jesus Himself.[12] The interactive and parallel use of words and language referencing God's ordering of both His realms should not be missed or discounted. Whether they know it or not, government officials—all of them—serve at God's pleasure and are His ministers.

---

10 Romans 13:1–7. Italics are emphasis added by the author.

11 The premier and infamous example of this is John Howard Yoder, *The Politics of Jesus*, 2nd ed. (Eerdmans, 1972, 1994), 199–209. While I am quite critical of Yoder's refusal to acknowledge government as God's good servant, I believe in this same chapter of his book that he does a superb job of expressing the centrality and significance of Paul's directive for Christians to live in submission to government.

12 Romans 15:16; Hebrews 1:7; and Hebrews 8:2, respectively.

The second observation to be made about Romans 13 is the unequivocal directive that Christians must submit to earthly authority. Paul allows no exceptions, no caveats, no restrictions, no mitigating criteria, no implicit qualifiers; he simply asserts the bald command: Be subject to governing authorities. Again, Paul doubles down on this idea, issuing the admonition twice with the same Greek verb, *hypotassō*. This word, so important in the New Testament, comes from the root, *taxis*, which means "order, design, or arrangement." To be *hypo taxis* is to be under order—to be in the place where you are supposed to be according to the plan or design; it means to be in submission, to be in the right spot, taking one's place in God's arrangement, giving oneself freely to the way that God has established things to be. Given the Western world's abject fear and loathing of any form of submission, Paul's directive sounds altogether odd and even offensive. But the Enlightenment, with its celebration of individualism and democratic ideals, does not blunt and should not twist the Christian truth that animates Paul's words. It is worth remembering that such Christian exhortation is a challenge to every fallen sinner in every time and place who lives helplessly turned in on self. Paul's readers in Rome likely also marveled at the apostle's sweeping insistence on submission to rulers. Luther, who read his Bible and believed God's Word of truth, unreservedly embraced Paul's exhortation, even when it was decidedly unpopular to do so.

At this stage, it is vitally essential to pause and make unmistakably clear that the divine creation and endorsement of government does not mean divine affirmation or approval of all that governments and their leaders do. It is more than possible, indeed likely, that a man may be at once God's chosen servant and at the same time and in the same office utterly evil and opposed to God. The same Caesar declared by Paul as God's *diakonos* can commit gross immorality, horrible injustice, torture and kill Christians, and even execute Paul himself. This is not in the least ironic and would not have surprised or perplexed Paul; it is merely and predictably the reality that results when God's good design is first perverted and subsequently managed and staffed by sinful, broken humans. Christians who rightly hold to the teaching of the two realms operate with neither illusions nor naivete. And Christians committed to the truth of the two realms most certainly do not blindly affirm, support, and obey whatever government or ruler is currently in power on the premise that God has told them to submit. As Luther knew and clearly taught, a Christian "submits himself for the sake of love to magistrates, also to their wicked laws, and to everything else in this present life—even, if need be, to burden and danger."[13] The burden and danger are all the more acute when it becomes necessary to "obey God rather than men."[14] Christians who submit themselves to their appointed rulers and yet refuse to obey those rulers when they demand what is sinful will necessarily follow the road of submission, even to government-enforced martyrdom, rather than violate God's ordered plan for His creation. So, within the teaching of the two realms, there is an absolute need for submission and yet this submission does not endorse or even imply a corollary demand for absolute obedience, much less unflagging patriotism and jingoistic nationalism. Those unable to make this distinction have compounded untold suffering and harm to human lives and to the church's faithful confession and witness. That this reality is not confined to a regrettable historical interlude or occasional past failure but continues as a constant and present threat should command the focused attention of all who seek faithfully to follow Christ.

What Paul declared with such clarity is precisely echoed also by the apostle Peter. Indeed, the fact that 1 Peter 2 makes essentially the same argument and supporting points as Romans 13,

---

13 AE 26:12.

14 Acts 5:29.

even using the same word for *submission* and yet with a very differently structured presentation, strongly reinforces the centrality of these basic truths about the temporal realm. Peter also pulls no punches and leaves little room for evasion or nuance:

> Be subject for the Lord's sake to every human institution, whether it be to the emperor as supreme, or to governors as sent by him to punish those who do evil and to praise those who do good. For this is the will of God, that by doing good you should put to silence the ignorance of foolish people. Live as people who are free, not using your freedom as a cover-up for evil, but living as servants of God. Honor everyone. Love the brotherhood. Fear God. Honor the emperor.[15]

Peter next provides his readers with specific direction for slaves in relation to their masters, but as his exhortation continues by holding up Jesus as the perfect example, it is difficult to imagine he expects his obedient hearers to be only the particular segment of readers who were slaves. Peter's words of exhortation resonate with just the sort of expansive and normative tone that we are used to hearing from Paul and Jesus when they offer teaching intended for all Christians. Peter urges his readers:

> But if when you do good and suffer for it you endure, this is a gracious thing in the sight of God. For to this you have been called, because Christ also suffered for you, leaving you an example, so that you might follow in His steps. He committed no sin, neither was deceit found in His mouth. When He was reviled, He did not revile in return; when

---

15 1 Peter 2:13–17.

> He suffered, He did not threaten, but continued entrusting Himself to Him who judges justly.[16]

Christians do not rebel against authority, even when that authority is acting in opposition to the will of God, who granted them their authority, even when that authority is acting unjustly, even when it is threatening harm—and yet, at the same time, Christians do *not* merely capitulate and succumb to the ruling powers in meek or misguided compliance. There is a marked difference also between rebellion and vocal and visible but nonviolent resistance. And there is great comfort for those who stand on God's truth and resist injustice, sin, and evil while still submitting to the wrong and wicked exercise of civil authority. Peter concludes his ardent exhortation and offer of Jesus as example with a delicious declaration of the Gospel delivered by Jesus, the Savior:

> He Himself bore our sins in His body on the tree, that we might die to sin and live to righteousness. By His wounds you have been healed. For you were straying like sheep, but have now returned to the Shepherd and Overseer of your souls.[17]

God's people live peacefully, righteously, and confidently in God's world—in spite of what the citizens and rulers of that world might threaten and do to harm them. Christians know God's grace and promises delivered in Christ and so fear no human or earthly power. They joyfully fulfill the work God gives them to do according to His way of operating in both the spiritual and temporal realms of His creation.

The two realms, it should by now be clear, are not a Lutheran invention or an alien paradigm imposed on Scripture or Christian

---

16 1 Peter 2:20–23.

17 1 Peter 2:24–25.

doctrine in order to advance some political or personal agenda. The two realms are simply the description of the way that God works in His rebellious and broken creation to bring it back into a right relationship with Himself. Having explored the foundational realities of the teaching and some of the critical interactions and relationships between this teaching and other aspects of Christian confession, we are now ready to consider in more detail the precise working of the two realms in our world today.

Chapter 2
The Two Realms in Action

There is a long-standing complaint that theologians become so obsessed and preoccupied with theological prolegomena that they never have time, energy, or space left to do the actual work of theology. The criticism is fair, and I fear that I am becoming guilty of this myself. So, it is time—probably long past time—to move from situating and preparing for a right understanding of the teaching of the two realms to the actual work of presenting and explaining the teaching as it stands. With the goal of doing the work in sight, I offer one more prefatory observation about the work itself. Systematic theology is the endeavor to offer anyone who is interested, both believers and unbelievers, descriptions of God's reality that are both faithful and helpful. Naturally, God's reality encompasses metaphysical truth about the universe, eternity, and human and nonhuman being, but it also includes every last part of the immediate, temporal, and thoroughly mundane and routinely familiar world that surrounds each of us each day. The teaching of the two realms is perhaps more interested in this latter, earthly reality, though it certainly presumes and articulates aspects of the former as necessary. My purpose is to give a way of discussing and thinking about the vitally important and endlessly relevant component of our lives that unfolds in this present world; accordingly, I will focus most of my attention on the temporal realm. Above all, what I present will strive to conform to what God actually says and does, with the hope that the lives we live can be better—that is, more faithful to the God who created the world and put us here to care for it. As noted, the specific interest of the two realms is to offer a way of understanding and appreciating the two quite different yet entirely complementary and compatible ways that God has of working in His fallen creation that He continues to love and win back to Himself. With all of that in mind, the work can begin.

The Scope of Each Realm

We are living in a world that God is actively ruling and redeeming. This basic truth is universal, extending, of course, even to those who do not acknowledge God's reality and are ignorant, whether willfully or not, of God and His plans. The world around us, God's own creation, is very good, designed and brought into reality through God's powerful Word. It is a stunningly beautiful, endlessly fascinating, bewilderingly complex, intricately interconnected world that captivates, comforts, inspires, nurtures, and defines us in our human existence. God's masterwork of creation is extraordinary. And it is also fallen. It is corrupted, perverted, and twisted so that it now operates at cross purposes with and in opposition to God's perfect plan. Tragically, this sad reality was imposed on the creation by the very creature God had designed to be the manager and steward of this world.

Yet even a fallen creation still matters to God. The Gospel is the incredible story of God's plan to redeem and restore His lost and broken creation through the work of His own Son, the Word made flesh. That story unfolds as God works to preserve, reclaim, love, restore, and finally glorify His creation. He does this work through the two realms. The realm that is centered on telling the Gospel story and extending the forgiving, restoring, and re-creating grace won by Jesus is called the spiritual realm. The realm that is occupied with upholding and enhancing right now the proper functioning of the creation according to God's design is called the temporal realm. These are the terms that Luther consistently used, and they still serve the purpose. Westerners must resist the impulse to privilege the spiritual over the temporal as somehow superior or more significant. Temporal does not mean unimportant, trivial, or only temporary; it simply means timebound in distinction from the spiritual realm that operates apart from time constraints. There is nothing inherently negative about the temporal realm—in fact, the physical creation or temporal realm is the object of God's activity in the spiritual realm. The two realms have also been distinguished as God's right-hand realm, the spiritual, and God's left-hand realm, the temporal. While this terminology was used only rarely by Luther, the image evoked is quite potent and helpful. The idea of God's two hands vividly conveys the truth that both realms belong to God and that He is the active presence and force at work in each. The two hands imagery also reinforces the compatibility and cooperation that exists as each hand of God works with the other to accomplish God's purposes both presently and ultimately.

God's left-hand, temporal realm is focused on this present world and the way that it and all its inhabitants function. It involves government, certainly, but in truth, government is merely the institution established by God to help oversee, organize, and protect the creation's right functioning. There is so much more to the purview of the temporal realm than only the small portion claimed by government. The temporal realm includes marriage and child-rearing, art and industry, sports and game-playing, work and production, music and linguistics, gardening and farming, medicine and machinery, architecture and apparel, and culture and cuisine. The temporal realm encompasses every aspect of the lives lived by all the people of this world in every place in this world. From the perspective of what we know through our senses, it is all encompassing. And there is nothing sinister, nasty, or negative about God's temporal realm. Every Christian rightly lives and prospers, serving their neighbors and honoring God within the temporal realm.

Neither is there any reason that government itself should be considered as somehow evil or odious. Nothing in Scripture indicates that government is a fallback, alternate plan reluctantly established by God to mitigate the problem of sin and evil. Rather, government should be understood as God's arrangement for human creatures better to fulfill their responsibilities in the world together as stewards. In other words, even in a world without sin, there would still be a need for order and planning and execution of ideas—especially in a world busily occupied with the work of humans being fruitful and multiplying according to the first great commission from God. In a fallen creation, however, that oversight also now involves bearing the sword of authority to serve as the enforcer of justice. So, according to God's plan, in a fallen world, government is responsible to curtail the effects of sin, aid the victims of various afflictions, and discourage, thwart, stop, and punish those bent on doing evil.

While all of the temporal realm business and action of the world is churning along according to God's good plan, God is simultaneously at work in His spiritual realm. In the right-hand, spiritual realm, the center of attention is not this present life and the responsibilities and relationships that define and enrich that life; rather, the focus is on each relationship between each individual creature and his or her Creator. The temporal realm concerns itself with horizontal realities creature-to-creature, and the spiritual realm centers on the vertical realities Creator-to-creature and vice versa. The institution established to oversee and administer the spiritual realm is, of course, the church, which is entrusted with the means of grace that deliver God's Gospel to sinners to bring them into, and keep them in, a right relationship with their Creator. This Gospel work of the church is essential because the Gospel fully accomplished and delivered through the life, death, and resurrection of Christ is the one and only way that fallen human creatures shattered and condemned by sin can ever hope to find peace with God and so live with confidence, certainty, and even joy in this life. Only the good news of a right relationship with God can provide an answer to the terror of death, sin's devastating wages, and save sinful humans from the hell they deserve.

The differences between the temporal and spiritual realms could not be more dramatic. In the left-hand realm, relationships are built and maintained only by the energy and effort expended by creatures; in the right-hand realm, on the other hand, a relationship with God is established and kept right only by the gracious action of God. The temporal realm is the place where creatures rightly pursue the active righteousness of good works. The spiritual realm is where the passive righteousness of the Gospel is delivered to those who receive it in faith. The marked difference and yet extensive correspondence and easy cooperation between the two realms are manifest in a number of ways. This becomes especially clear when the two realms are considered in parallel to each other. Indeed, working through some of the specific distinctions and yet commonalities between realms in a back-and-forth parallel way provides an excellent method of better understanding each realm and their interrelationship. What follows, then, will be just such a consideration of each realm under a series of topics or key areas of interest related to each realm and how they work.

Jurisdiction and Administration

With regard to the foundations, we have established that the left-hand realm is all about the proper functioning of this material world in which we live; and the right-hand realm is all about the relationship we have with the God who created this world and who will judge each human being and issue an eternal verdict about the sort of creatures we are. Each operates within a specific jurisdiction according to the plan of God, who establishes both realms and is thoroughly invested in both realms. This foundational distinction relates also to the basic distinction of Law and Gospel. In the temporal realm, the Law is critical as it discloses God's will for the way that He desires His creation to work and guides creatures to live as God intends. In the spiritual realm, the proclamation of the Gospel is the essential thing, since only God's grace given in Christ makes it possible for us to escape God's righteous condemnation of our inevitable failure to live fully according to His good plan, the Law.

Within each of the two realms, God has established leaders to administer that realm's activity. In the left-hand realm are the governmental rulers and layer upon layer upon layer of bureaucrats and advisers to assist them. In Luther's day, these rulers responsible for the management of the temporal realm were dubbed princes—the same term used by Luther's contemporary Machiavelli in his notorious treatise, *The Prince*. A temporal ruler's title is not particularly important. Whether they are princes, kings, emperors, dictators, presidents, sultans, prime ministers, governors, mayors, or any other term or name is immaterial. Neither does it make much difference exactly how the ruler came to wield power. Whether by election, acclamation, heredity, treachery, revolution, or even a coup d'état, the ruler exercising the controls of civil power grasps the sword—in other words, the necessary authority to rule—because God has granted or allowed it. Whoever they are, whatever they are called, and however they rule, rulers hold their position of authority at the will and direction of God and are to serve according to His plan and purposes for the temporal or civil realm. Whether and to what extent a Christian may question, challenge, or reject the legitimacy and authority of a government or its ruler will be considered more fully in the next chapter as one of the special problems confronted when thinking in terms of two realms. It can be admitted already, though, that one of the real-world challenges of following a two realms approach is that there are times and circumstances when it is not easy to identify with confidence exactly who it is that qualifies as God's chosen authority.

To some extent, this problem also holds in the spiritual realm of the church, which is precisely why the Augsburg Confession takes pains to spell out precisely the criteria for a pastor to be a pastor: "Concerning church order they teach that no one should teach publicly in the church or administer the sacraments unless properly called."[1] The objective of this brief article was to curtail the promulgation and curb the influence of self-appointed preachers, prophets, or teachers who, for whatever motive, would peddle and proffer their insights and teaching as the authoritative truth about God. And, if the presence of such pretenders, dreamers, charlatans, and deceivers could not be stopped altogether, at least the faithful church could disavow any connection to the illegitimate preacher and his lies and so protect faithful believers from being tricked or lulled into heterodoxy or even heresy. God's chosen men, put into their office through the work of Christ's church, were bound to the oversight and discipline of the church. This assured the truth and faithfulness of their teaching and, in the vertical realm, provided people with the confidence that what their pastor preached and taught was consistent with God's truth, normed by God's will that was made known in Christ and recorded as the written text of the Bible. Each realm, then, has its own peculiar institution to accomplish God's purposes in its respective realm, and those institutions are administered and directed by God's appointed leaders—those who hold a divine office, or *Amt*, that is a position of responsible leadership and authority established by God.

1 AC XIV, Latin.

THE TOOLS OF THE TRADE AND THE OBJECTIVES

Each distinct officeholder, pastor and prince, has been given peculiar tools appropriate to the task he is to fulfill. Tempting as it is to grant summarily the government's use of the sword to enforce the rule of law with a few quick sentences and then comfortably settle into a much longer and very familiar presentation of the church's Gospel tools of Word and Sacrament, I will take the opposite approach. My intent is not to diminish the essential, indeed eternal, significance of the church's work but to affirm quickly but definitively the reams of material already available that ably presents and extols this Gospel work and then invest more space to thinking about the work and tools of God's other realm. Gospel proclamation work delivers resurrection life; that work is, of course, the marvelous privilege of the church and her pastors. Using the Spirit-animated tools of the preached Word and the tangible location of that living Word through the Sacraments of Baptism and the Lord's Supper, the church delivers God's greatest gifts to people desperate for grace. The particular individual entrusted with fulfilling the Gospel office of pastor is not significant—it is the work he does and the gifts he delivers that matter. Similarly, the extent or nature of the pastor's training for this work is neither specified nor mandated. Issues of character and aptitude carry far greater significance.[2] It is the action of God in putting a man into this office that counts. As articulated by Article 14 of the Augsburg Confession, God uses His church to call a man into this work, and that man then serves with the authority of Christ Himself. He works in Christ's name, delivering Christ's gifts: forgiveness of sins and the favor of God.

Gospel work is holy work done for the sake of God's creatures to put them in a right relationship with their Creator and make them heirs of life. In a word, this is the work of justification.

---

2 1 Timothy 3:1–7; Titus 1:5–9.

The gift and its means of delivery are confessed and celebrated in Articles 4 and 5 of the Augsburg Confession:

> Furthermore, it is taught that we cannot obtain forgiveness of sin and righteousness before God through our merit, work, or satisfactions, but that we receive forgiveness of sin and become righteous before God out of grace for Christ's sake through faith when we believe that Christ has suffered for us and that for his sake our sin is forgiven and righteousness and eternal life are given to us. For God will regard and reckon this faith as righteousness in his sight, as St. Paul says in Romans 3[:21–26] and 4[:5].
>
> To obtain such faith God instituted the office of preaching, giving the gospel and the sacraments. Through these, as through means, he gives the Holy Spirit who produces faith, where and when he wills, in those who hear the gospel. It teaches that we have a gracious God, not through our merit but through Christ's merit, when we so believe.[3]

The tight connection between the right-hand realm's proclamation of the Gospel and the man appointed to do that work is evident. And so, according to God's good plan, sinful human creatures receive the grace of God and are restored to live as God's people now and into eternity. This is the holy work of the church and her pastor.

The prince also does holy work. While he is not charged with delivering the Gospel—and in fact in the context of his office in the temporal realm, he should ordinarily resist the urge to engage

---

3 AC IV 1–3; V 1–3.

in such Gospel proclamation—he is charged with upholding God's Law. His work is holy because it is done within and according to the will and purpose of God. For the sake of God's creation, the prince has been charged with administering the interactions and business that make up ordinary life in the temporal realm. For this reason, he strives to facilitate human flourishing, endeavors to maintain justice, labors to curtail disobedience, rebellion, and evil or what the church would simply and broadly label as sin, and attends to the needs of those who endure, to various degrees, the manifold afflictions imposed by this broken world's groanings and thrashings—whether inflicted directly by other people or by the innumerable natural disasters that occur in a creation languishing under the curse provoked by man's sin. Obviously, the prince is responsible for a great deal more than merely thwarting evil. Yet, in a good creation now shattered by sin, evil certainly abounds, and so the pressing task of the prince must be, whenever possible, to stem the spread of evil and diminish its ill effects. To fulfill this harsh but necessary work, the prince has been entrusted with the sword.

Paul's choice of imagery is hardly accidental. The sword was the tool of warfare. It was used to threaten, to coerce, to shed blood, and to kill. Hence, the sword was the unmistakable symbol for power and force in the temporal world. "At the point of a sword" is a standard but pregnant phrase that to this day never fails to communicate a precise message. When God gives the sword to the prince, He gives him the authority to stop evil, uphold justice, and encourage good behavior, all backed by the point of the sword. While the sword may not be the ideal tool for every princely task—as we will consider more fully below—it is a remarkably effective tool in directly combating and stopping evil. Dead men not only tell no tales; they do no further evil. And the threat of imprisonment and death does offer a certain level of deterrence. Given the bloody realities and the inherent force implicit with the sword, it should not be surprising that the very mention of the word generates a great deal of angst and perplexity for Christians who rightly hold to the inherent nonviolence of Christ's realm and are unable to reconcile God sanctioning the sword with Jesus' command to sheath the sword. The problem, of course, lies in the failure to recognize the legitimacy and significance of God's two realms at work in this world.

It may well seem patently absurd that any follower of Christ could ever tolerate, much less practice, the brutal force of the sword regardless the end result of that force. Yet the teaching of the two realms seems to lead us into precisely this disconcerting reality. It should be remembered, however, that this is a reality taught in the Bible and a reality that the two realms paradigm actually helps bring into sharper focus. The teaching of the two realms does not create the problem. On the contrary, Luther's teaching of the two complementary realms of God's work in the world actually clarifies and resolves the problem of Christians commending the use of the sword. Without the benefit of the two realms as a guide, it is inevitable that Christians will be perplexed by Peter's and Paul's steady endorsement of Caesar and his facility in using the sword provided by God. Christians who are constrained by an unfounded and largely unconsidered rejection of the two realms paradigm often have great difficulty conceding any place in their understanding of God's activity in the temporal realm for the destructive, indeed lethal, power of the sword. And so it is precisely at this juncture that the two realms distinction demonstrates both its fidelity to the written text of the Bible (which is certainly the primary concern) and its utility for making sense of the sometimes death-dealing work of the temporal realm.

In a world that has been thoroughly infiltrated and utterly corrupted by sin and its lurking and ubiquitous evil, the sword is the essential tool. It is not justified merely by pragmatics, but it is blessed by the explicit direction of the Holy Spirit, who inspired the apostle Paul.[4] While the world awaits its full and final redemption and restoration at the return of Christ in glory, evil needs to be kept in check and not allowed free rein. Hence, God's provision of the sword to the one responsible for the management of the temporal realm. The necessary but often brutally nasty work of battling evil with the sword is mandated by God, who establishes government, at least in part, to wage this campaign and directs the office of prince to execute it. The work is often a grim and bloody business but is rightly necessitated not by the ambition or bloodlust of rulers but in response to the lawless rebellion of sinful humans. This governmental use of lethal force against foreign and domestic evildoers is not justified by a noble motivation or the intended outcome of greater peace and security, nor is it justified because it resonates with a human sense of fairness. The sole justification for the prince's use of the sword can be nothing more than the fact that God has directed this work that is carried out in accord with God's standard of justice. Without a clear understanding of the two distinct ways that God works in His two realms, it will always be virtually impossible to reconcile God's gifting of the sword with Jesus' demand for nonretaliation and the disavowal of individual rights and autonomy.[5]

While government and its office of prince employ the negative and destructive force of the sword to thwart evil plans and practices, they also work constructively with positive force to mitigate the impact of evil inflicted by sin and Satan at work in the world. It is quite right for governments and their rulers to organize, fund, and carry out relief for those who have been run down by rampant human evil or those who have simply been caught up in the storms and chaos of a cursed creation. This edifying and uplifting work can take many forms, at times offering rescue and sustenance for

---

4 Romans 13:1–4.

5 Matthew 5:38–42; Luke 9:23–26.

those who suffer the immediate consequences of evil and at other times working strategically to curtail the rise of evil before it starts or curb the spread of its devastating effects whether by funding medical research, promoting education, creating entrepreneurial opportunities, or even by encouraging and supporting the Gospel work of the church. All of these activities certainly fall within the parameters of earthly rulers "prais[ing] those who do good," as Peter put it (1 Peter 2:14).

It is also fully within the scope of those temporal rulers to offer solutions or at least ways forward to counter all the ways that sin infects and perverts the right operation of families, business, education, industry, science, the arts, and every other human endeavor. The mandate to wield the sword is not only limited to fighting back the foreign invader or jailing the neighborhood thief. It also rightly extends to finding and fostering ways to address and rectify the evil of injustice, whether a single instance toward an individual or a generational blight against an entire ethnicity. The sword cuts, shatters, breaks, and destroys, and the work of a faithful prince must include such destructive tasks, but the prince's work is not conducted only with the sword. According to God's plan, there is also much room for creative, constructive, and upbuilding work. In fact, such positive endeavors are expected as a critical responsibility of temporal rulers.

The sword is the essential tool and a fitting symbol of the office responsible for the temporal realm, but it is hardly the only tool. As noted earlier, government does not exist only to counteract evil, alleviate the suffering of evil, or create circumstances that stem the growth of evil. Altogether apart from the necessary work imposed on temporal rulers by the pervasive presence of evil in a fallen world, it is important to remember that temporal authority also serves the essential task of organizing and managing the ongoing and defining purpose of humans to work and keep, or cultivate and manage, the creation. In other words, government exists not only because evil runs wild and must be countered but also to facilitate the right functioning of the creation itself. Government is in the business of enhancing the smooth operation of the creation.

The Best Form of Government

Clearly, there are myriad ways that this oversight and organization can be duly accomplished with virtually any form of government allowing for successful completion of the basic governmental task of oversight and management of the creation. At the same time, though, living now in a world corrupted by sin and ruled by officeholders also thoroughly corrupted by sin, history, and lived experience have made abundantly clear that the ideal situation of rulers exhibiting wholly selfless guidance and disinterested direction for the good of the creation will forever remain an unattainable aspiration. Frustration and impatience with any and all government is therefore inevitable, and governments and the humans that run them have earned their universal and dubious status as legendary tropes of inefficiency, self-promotion, and corruption. Given the brokenness of the world and its inhabitants, it should surprise no one that governments frequently and categorically fail to fulfill their divine mandate. Nevertheless, precisely these flawed and failed institutions and their administrators are affirmed as God's chosen tools and servants.

These civil servants are God's servants and are to rule according to God's will. From the perspective of Christian confession, judgment on the success or failure of a general form of government or of a specific administration or prince is never limited to questions of bare pragmatics or effectiveness or even personal character. Whether or not a ruler can ably manage human behavior and curb evil is critically important, of course, and, for good or ill, the visibility and stature of their office certainly provides an example; but from a Christian perspective, there is a more foundational standard to be considered. Not only is it important that a ruler get things done or serve as a worthy exemplar to their subjects, but that ruler must be doing things that conform to God's will. This concept is too often absent or trivialized when Christians engage in reflection or discussion on the two realms but deserves to be emphasized. Scripture makes clear that the authority of every government is derived from God and that every government is accountable to God for the administration of their office. In other words, God's will is normative for every government in every place and in every time, period.

Obviously, the reality that prevails is typically diametrically opposed to this Christian standard—governments operate with all manner of motives and objectives other than upholding God's Law. Nevertheless, the criteria for Christian judgment about what constitutes a good government or civil ruler must always be the creational law established by God for the right functioning of the world. Where exactly that law is revealed and how one confidently discerns God's will for the functioning of the world pushes us into old, complicated, and often contentious discussions about revelation, reason, and the natural law and its content and accessibility. A properly complete consideration of that discussion surpasses the limits of this little book; nevertheless, a few key points can be made.

As the Creator, Sustainer, and Lord of the universe, God established every law and rule that directs every part of its operation. God's perfect plan and direction is aptly called the natural or, as I prefer, the creational law. Human sin corrupted God's plan that binds and guides the creation, but it did not eradicate it. Every creature, including every human creature, has been and remains perfectly designed to conform to and live within the Creator's rule and will that surround and encounter us at every moment. God's Law that suffuses reality is readily apparent and so available to any and all honest observers and thinkers—as the archives of philosophy and human learning readily attest. And yet, because humans live now in their fallen state as rebels against their Creator and refuse to yield to His lordship or acknowledge His will, they are quite able willfully and petulantly to ignore, reject, and deny God's creational law and replace His authority with their own—again, as the archives of philosophy and human learning readily attest. Human history traces the vacillating and often fascinating but inevitably tragic trajectory of man's interminable and inescapable efforts to navigate the interface between the unyielding reality of God's Law and man's often grandiose but invariably failed ventures to live apart from that Law and instead heed his own desires and schemes.

Corroborated and articulated explicitly in the Decalogue and the whole of Scriptures, the creational law is accessible to all temporal realm rulers. That creational law is the criteria according to which God intends every government to establish positive law, determine justice, and execute their rule. God's Law is also the criteria by which the quality or success of rulers and their governing must now and ultimately will be judged. Christians should hold all governments and civil rulers to no lower standard than God's will; and the pastor, the church's authoritative officeholder, is fully within his jurisdiction—indeed, is expected—to remind civil authorities of their accountability to God's Law. Odd as this may sound to those accustomed to bifurcating the two realms, this government accountability to God's Law and God's representative is consistent with a right understanding of the two realms. It is precisely this right understanding that has led faithful ecclesiastical leaders throughout history to challenge and rightly resist unjust and ungodly actions of rulers—whether Ambrose rebuking Emperor Theodosius I or Bonhoeffer subverting the rule of Hitler. Some practical reflection on this challenging work will be offered in the next chapter. Finally, it should be noted that civil authorities who do govern in conformity with God's will discover the good fruit of living in tune with the grain of the universe and will reap the benefits not only for themselves but for their people.

Considered in the light of the enduring standard of the creational law and the devastating brokenness of sin, it is quite true that while any form of government may be able to accomplish God's purpose for temporal rule, some are better than others—or perhaps more accurately, some are less contemptible or perhaps less liable to abuse than others. So which government is best? I often declare that I am personally inclined to advocate for a benevolent dictatorship and can make a solid case for its many advantages—but, of course, the one, probably unsurpassable, difficulty lies with the benevolent part! Benevolent dictators are a wonderful theory, but in reality always, and all too soon, devolve into simple, power-hungry dictators. Lord Acton was not the least bit unfair or even cynical in his observation about the nefarious and absolute correlation between power and corruption. This harsh reality explains the attractiveness of a federal republic system, or any form of government or earthly administration premised on layers of checks and balances that curtail the location of temporal power in any one person or place. Deeply suspicious of humanity's ability to attain and retain true altruism and benevolence, democratic republics seek to balance and check the concentration or cultivation of power in any one place or person. The naturally resultant gridlock, inefficiency, craven mediocrity, and grindingly ponderous progress of such democratic and republican governments are perhaps small prices to pay to curb the unbridled exercise of nimble and swift power in the hands of one or a few.

The twofold reality of God's authoritative creational law and the definitive brokenness of man also sheds light on economic truths and the pros and cons of various systems. Once again, experience and history are instructive, but in this case, from the perspective of a creational law standard, it is more difficult to assert the clear superiority or advantages of one system over another.

Both free market laissez-faire capitalism and centrally planned, micromanaged, government-controlled economies are liable to excesses, abuses, and failure to conform to God's will. In spite of personal preferences, or patriotic commitments, Christians should be able to acknowledge that neither capitalism nor socialism can be deemed either inherently incapable or ideally suited as systems for upholding and extending God's will for the functioning of His creation. Both have strengths and weaknesses that can be used for great good or exploited for great harm.

The Goals and Ends of Each Realm

Every person, every creature, every institution must operate with a specific *raison d'être*. Without a reason for being or an end, goal, or purpose—that is, a *telos*—to provide direction, clarity, and significance for decisions and strategies in both the short and the long term, human creatures and their institutions will flounder and fail. So, the final consideration when looking in parallel at God's two realms is the precise *telos* that animates and guides each.

It should by now be all but self-evident, but to be clear, the objective of the temporal realm is the entire creation functioning as God intended it to function. Obviously, this is a lofty and, because of the curse of the fall, an utterly unattainable goal. Yet it is important to see the big picture in order to rightly orient the work done in the present. Done well, government continually should be asking itself if it is aiding the care and cultivation of the world and the thriving of the creatures who live in it. The necessary guidance on the ordering and prioritizing of this work remains, as just argued, the enduring reality of God's creational law. In this light, it is entirely appropriate, then, to assert that the *telos* of a government should be justice—that is, justice according to God's revealed will. Justice is defined by God and not by people. Every decision, every action, every policy of the government should aim at upholding and extending the reach of justice to every part of the creation. Clearly, this leaves a great deal of latitude to how this might be accomplished, but it certainly invites the possibility of an "activistic" government that seeks to ameliorate the suffering of evil while also promoting the cultivation of human flourishing.

Interestingly—and perhaps provocatively—it could well be argued that the goal of the right-hand, spiritual realm is precisely the same as that of the left-hand, temporal realm: the whole of creation operating in the fullness of all that God ever intended it to be. Jesus came to seek and to save the lost, to redeem, rescue, and restore the entire creation so that it would no longer groan in the futility of the curse of sin but delight to be what God created it to be.[6] On the Last Day, God's resurrected people will delight to be part of the glorious new heaven and the new earth that God will unveil. Creation will at last push to its *telos* and will be all that God had always planned for it to be.[7] This is the ultimate goal of the spiritual realm, one that it will reach and fully realize because God will bring it to pass through the preaching of the Gospel that leads to resurrection and eternal life.

This means that the immediate, short-term goal of the spiritual realm is the proclamation of the Gospel of Jesus Christ for the salvation of fallen, sinful people. In a word, the spiritual realm aims at justification. As I have done throughout this brief volume, I'll once again give short shrift to the theological side of the two realms and forgo any attempt to offer a full picture of the height, the breadth, and the depth of the marvel and delirious delight that is the doctrine of justification. As Luther learned, the Gospel of Jesus is God's greatest gift to sinners. Hopelessly cut off from the Creator, compelled to spend their lives striving to justify themselves as human beings worthy of life and love not only to other

6 Luke 19:10; Romans 8:18–25.

7 Revelation 21:1–5.

creatures but to themselves, and always ultimately incapable of success, humans need what only God can give. And through the life, death, and resurrection of Jesus, He gives it. Through His earthly ministry, Jesus justified the creation, and now through the Word preached and the Sacraments delivered, He justifies one sinner at a time and makes them His own. Justification means freedom from condemnation, release from the horror of hell, new meaning and purpose in life now, power to fight against the brokenness of sin, and anticipation of resurrected life in the new heaven and new earth. Justification is the *telos* of the church.

COOPERATION WITHOUT CONFUSION

With a sharp picture of the two realms in view, all that remains is to articulate precisely the lively, complementary, and mutually reinforcing relationship that rightly exists between the two realms. Both realms are God's realms. They are not inherently at odds or antagonistic. Of course, since sin cripples and perverts all of creation, it also invades both realms, complicating and compromising the right functioning of each as well as their mutual interrelationship. But it is not just the temporal realm that is shot through with sin—the spiritual realm is as well. Yet God still uses both of these realms administered by fallen humans to do His work. And they do this work together. The church delights to see government functioning as God intends, bringing order and justice to creation, and so affirms it when it does this work, and the church calls it to do better when it falls short. Likewise, a government operating as God intends will be eager to see the church carrying out her work of justifying people and will support the church in that work however it can. This is how the two realms are intended to work. That their interactions and interrelations fall horribly short of this standard is reason for lament and pleas for God's grace, but not for despair. Again, Christians are not shocked by sin's inroads into the creation. Yet, even when government openly rejects God's truth and order for this creation and defies God's Law, the church continues to recognize that, whenever possible, it works with and in support of the government and its God-given purpose. This is the idea captured in the dictum *cooperation without confusion*. This expression of the truth points out the mutual collaboration that should exist between the realms but also warns against the error of collapsing the two realms into a single unity. Each realm should keep in clear view what it is and is not trying to accomplish and focus on that task, but whenever possible, each should also willingly support and aid the other realm in its work. They cooperate but remain distinct.

The same idea can be expressed from the other direction as *distinction without divorce*. Stating the concept this way reminds those who are eager to build a wall of separation between the two realms that they are meant to work in tandem with one another as God's two hands and not be bifurcated into mutually repellant, sealed silos. Keeping the cooperation without confusion and distinction without divorce dictums clearly in mind and contemplating all the interactive parallel descriptions and assessments of each realm as presented in this chapter should provide essentially all that is needed to sort out any question or confusion about the right interface between the two realms. Remember the *telos*, the tools, the officeholders, the authority, and the scope of each realm; remember that, between the realms, there must be cooperation without confusion and distinction without divorce, and all the necessary truths are in place for a right way forward to come into focus.

Optimistic as I am about the usefulness and capability of the truths presented in this chapter for unraveling most of the difficulties encountered while trying to live faithfully in light of God's two realms, there are some peculiarly pervasive and often perplexing situations that face Christians living in the Western world of the twenty-first century. Exploring some of the most significant of those challenges along with some of the egregious ways that the right relationship between the two realms has been muddled and violated will be the work of the next chapter.

Chapter 3
The Axiom in Action

Expressing the basic idea of God's care for this world through two distinct realms is a relatively straightforward and simple exercise. Nevertheless, embracing that truth and using it faithfully as a guide for Christian interaction in the world appears to be anything but straightforward and simple. Christian people, even those within the Lutheran tradition who claim to follow the teaching, often seem to struggle with practicing good two realms theology. While there are, no doubt, difficult and complicated situations that confront Christians striving faithfully to follow Christ in a world bent on rebellion and rejection of God's grace and truth, operating according to the two realms actually is not especially difficult, and there is certainly nothing mysterious about it. It is basically a matter of paying attention to the jurisdiction of each realm, the objectives and tools of each realm, and then thinking through how best to further God's purpose in any given situation. I suspect that it is the final stipulation that often proves most beguiling, as Christians seem prone to lose sight of God's clearly revealed objectives and purposes for the world and mingle or substitute those ultimate purposes with goals and agendas that are considerably more earthbound, tribal, or crassly self-serving. An exhaustive listing, let alone consideration, of every possible way of muddling the teaching of the two realms and the misapplication of God's truth for the temporal and spiritual realms certainly lies well beyond the scope of this text. There are, though, a few overarching confusions of the two realms that recur with some regularity and so seem to be somewhat paradigmatic ways of getting things wrong.

The two most basic ways of making a mess of the distinction between God's realms both result from ignoring the twofold guiding axiom: cooperation without confusion and distinction without divorce. Problems arise on the one hand when the second half of the axiom is ignored and the spiritual realm and the temporal realm are driven apart, cordoned off, and isolated in hermetically sealed spheres that allow no overlap, interaction, or even influence to occur between the two. On the other hand are the difficulties and disasters that result when the first part of the axiom is violated, all distinction is ignored, and no effort is made to maintain the precise differences between God's work in the vertical dimension and His complementary but distinct activity in the horizontal arena. Though each error is in a sense the antithesis of the other, one collapsing the realms together and the other irreconcilably divorcing them, the resultant negative impact is often oddly similar. We'll first consider the disastrous way of getting the realms wrong by building an impregnable wall between them.

Divorcing the Realms

The problem of driving a wedge or building a wall between the realms manifests itself in many ways, some more obvious than others. Probably the most egregious, and in retrospect blatant, examples of this failure is the twentieth-century disaster referenced earlier, the church's utter failure during the rise and rule of Hitler's Third Reich. One need not endorse the charge that Hitler's path to tyranny was facilitated by Lutherans committed to a "doctrine of the two kingdoms" to acknowledge that the church in Germany did not fulfill its civil responsibility in responding to Hitler. Indeed, the reality is that it was not Luther's doctrine of the two realms that was at fault but the failure rightly to practice Luther's teaching that helped create the disaster that unfolded in Europe. While many Lutherans may have been culpable, Lutheran teaching itself was not at fault. The credibility of this claim is confirmed by men like Martin Niemöller, Hermann Sasse, and Dietrich Bonhoeffer who faithfully followed a path provided by the teaching of the two realms and resisted and defied the elected German dictator while so many of their countrymen, and ostensibly fellow Lutherans, simply capitulated to the lure of a strong temporal leader who promised a renewed and dominant nation. The case for this argument is ably presented by Uwe Siemon-Netto's book, *The Fabricated Luther*.[1] For now, it is enough to make clear that it was precisely the failure to follow Luther's teaching that led ordinary Christians to believe they could neatly separate their political lives as German citizens from their spiritual lives as believers in Christ and followers of His truth. By isolating their confession of Christ from their responsibility to care for their neighbors, their countrymen, and their fellow humans in the world around them, they found a way to excuse rhetoric, policies, behavior, and extraordinary crimes all diametrically at odds with the teachings of Jesus and His church.

The problem of the bifurcation of the realms lies in the failure to hold the inherent tension. This breakdown is exacerbated when earthly agendas and rulers are given precedence over the lordship of Christ, and Peter's dictum is grotesquely perverted into "We must obey men not God." While obedience to rulers is absolutely commanded, obedience to the rule of Christ is also commanded. And as Acts 5:29 makes explicit, when obedience to any earthly ruler contradicts obedience to Christ, there is nothing to debate or discuss. God's Word wins. Jesus is Lord. That Lutherans have so easily and tragically forsaken the lordship of Jesus to fawn over earthly rulers, hopes, and promises is an ugly stain not on Lutheranism's doctrine but on both her teachers and listeners who failed to uphold right teaching. Lessons of history must be

---

1 Uwe Siemon-Netto, *The Fabricated Luther: Refuting Nazi Connections and Other Modern Myths*, 3rd ed. (Concordia Publishing House, 2023).

remembered, of course, but the great tragedy of this inability to hold the realms together is that it is not an isolated historical mistake. The lure to take the easy route of segregating the realms into independent and unrelated parts of life continues into the present; indeed, the errant notion runs rampant in twenty-first-century America, especially among those inclined to advocate for typically conservative ways of operating. The resultant reticence on the part of followers of Christ to assert their Christian convictions and commitment to God's Law in the secular realm has been aptly dubbed quietism.

The challenge for Lutherans in an American context largely lies in the fact that the Constitution of the United States enshrines the separation of church and state. On the face of it, the nonestablishment, noninterference clause of the First Amendment seems to align neatly with the Lutheran distinction between the realms—which is precisely the problem. What appears as a perfect match is in reality anything but that. The Constitution's author, Thomas Jefferson, made clear that the stipulated separation should be enforced with an unyielding wall. This wall was portrayed as a boon to Christians concerned about government encroachment on their spiritual and religious lives, but it was also a less than subtle, but largely ignored, move to preempt any potential threats posed by the interference of religiously motivated citizens who might complicate the plans and ideals of serious, empirically grounded, and strictly rational thinkers and statesmen who could not be troubled with moral scruples, convictions, and ideals grounded not in Enlightenment convictions and confidence but in old texts and myths. The idea was simple: keep religion where it belongs in the heart, in the home, and in the church, but keep it out of the public square and the government. In that sphere, ardent Christians were to keep quiet about their specifically Christian commitments and convictions.

Of course, religious sentiment could serve as an ally and a prop for political authority as needed. Even today, "God bless America" is still accepted as the fitting thing to say at the end of a rousing political speech, and generic prayers on grand occasions continue to be granted a place in the proceedings. The reality, though, is that neither the church nor a natural law nor a lawgiver beyond the will of the people was afforded any place of influence or significance in the structure and shape of the American experiment. As long as the popular will of most Americans aligned with basic Christian moral tenets as it did for a couple centuries, the disjunction was barely noticed and hardly seemed to matter. But as the sordid fruit of the Enlightenment's exclusively anthropocentric agenda and hubris steadily increased, so did the height and breadth of the barricade between the spiritual and moral grounding of Christian confession and the standards and objectives of temporal government. The story of this cultural disintegration and resulting social and political crisis has been told many times over.[2]

Rather than collapsing into a nostalgic lament about the bad actors in the wider culture that have engineered the loss of Christian influence in America, for the present purpose, a far more productive route is to recognize the culpability of the church, her penchant for quietism, and so her failure to confront boldly government behavior at odds with God's creational law will for His world. This inability of the church to speak about God's will for His creation in meaningful ways can be traced to the unwillingness or perhaps incapacity of the church to engage the wider culture or its government for fear of breaching the supposedly sacred wall of separation between church and state or between the spiritual and

---

2 Three quite different but equally helpful tellings of this history are Patrick Deneen, *Why Liberalism Failed* (Yale University Press, 2019); Carl Trueman, *The Rise and Triumph of the Modern Self: Cultural Amnesia, Expressive Individualism, and the Road to Sexual Revolution* (Crossway, 2020); and James Davison Hunter, *Democracy and Solidarity: On the Cultural Roots of America's Political Crisis* (Yale University Press, 2024).

temporal aspects of their lives. The myth of a sharply demarcated separation of church and state is pervasive among all Americans, even those who confess faith in Christ and who seek faithfully to follow His will in their lives. The errant notion has been immortalized in the hackneyed slogan to which preachers are expected to subscribe: "Politics have no place in the pulpit." For Christians in America, it becomes far too easy simply to cordon off cherished spiritual truths from the hard and messy realities faced in a pluralistic and nationalistic culture and to allow and even encourage the temporal realm to operate without heeding God's will for the creation.

Examples of this failure abound. It can be seen when Christians are among the American citizens calling for the utter destruction of the nation's enemies seemingly oblivious to the most basic standards of God's justice as outlined in just war theory. The inability to surmount the separation of church and state is manifest when Christians who confess Jesus as the only way to peace with God and eternal life will in the name of the Enlightenment ideal of "religious liberty" ardently defend the "right" of people to believe in spiritual lies and false religions that will damn them. But in America, it is not polite or loving to suggest that someone's ideas or religion might lead them to hell. And the reticence to engage the culture with God's truth is evident when Christians are willing to defend a gay couple's "right" to marry or adopt children since it is a matter of "civil liberty and equality"—ideas which are grounded not in Christian confession or Holy Scripture but in Enlightenment precepts and Western conventions. Lulled into complacency and a spiritual lethargy by their notion that government should be left alone to take care of business, too many Christians have become oblivious to the glaring disjunction between God's will for this world and the policies and actions of their own nation. When they accept the wall of separation, they are sadly able, quite deftly, to justify this incongruity.

While the work of each of the two realms is certainly distinct and different, Christians must nevertheless tenaciously and tirelessly evaluate every aspect of temporal government rule according to the standard of God's Law. In their thinking about the civil realm, Christians should not apply a different standard that gives the government license to operate apart from God's Law for the creation under the misguided pretense that "this is just the temporal realm and Christian morality doesn't apply." God has one will for His creation, one Law to direct it.

The importance of Christians thinking the right way about God's standard for the temporal realm is not primarily about shifting governmental or bureaucratic behavior—which may well be quite unlikely—but about Christians living and thinking rightly and so providing a compelling and consistent witness of God's reality and His will for the right functioning of the world. When their government refuses to yield or even to listen, Christians will continue to speak God's truth and reality about the conduct of the temporal realm to themselves, to one another, to their neighbors, to the surrounding culture, and to their temporal rulers. In short, the premise is rather simple: In the temporal realm in which they honor and obey their civil rulers, Christians always should look, think, speak, and act as if their Lord is Jesus. For the sake of their primary task of providing a witness to the creation, this must be the guiding premise as they interact with the temporal realm and its authority. Living with Jesus as Lord will inevitably create a gulf between the Christian and the world around her; yet the Christian will never concede this divide. Instead, she will strive ceaselessly to bridge it with God's Law—and with God's Gospel.

Confusing the Realms

Understanding and practicing the two realms distinction is essential. When Christians fail to get this right, the casualties can be startling and catastrophically obvious to the world. But even when Christians confuse and obscure the distinct realms without glaring public repercussions, there are still deleterious consequences for the health, vitality, and witness of Christ's church and for the faith and life of Christians themselves. This is particularly the case when Christians go to the other extreme from bifurcating the realms and fall into the trap of confusing the realms into a toxic church-state mash-up. Once again, history provides compelling examples, or rather one very long and very pervasive example that spanned centuries becoming so much a part of church life that it was scarcely recognized as a deviation from God's truth.

There are various tellings of the story, of course, and wildly conflicting evaluations of its legacy, but the prevailing narratives all begin with Emperor Constantine working to preserve the newborn and novel unity he had created for his kingdom after converting (or capitulating) to the stubbornly expanding religion of Christianity. No longer struggling to the death against the ruthless force of Rome, the church was suddenly invited into the highest halls of power and temporal authority. The swift and surprising rapprochement between church and state has been interpreted as a great gift from God and Constantine canonized as a saint—and it has been lamented as a blight on the church and dubbed as Constantinianism, a moniker intended as anything but a compliment.

It is arguably better to savor the king's favor than to suffer his wrath and sword, and I would certainly prefer such a state for those I love. Nevertheless, on the whole, I'm inclined to agree with those who see the negative consequences of Constantinianism far outweighing any benefits. The state may well have gained a great deal on a number of fronts from its alignment with the church, including civil unity, cultural coherence, spiritual affirmation of political authority, and a strong moral underpinning for the populace. The church, however, did not fare so well, gaining earthly prestige, security, and wealth but gradually yet inevitably forfeiting the clarity and conviction of her unique witness to the Gospel of Christ. In short, for a tasty bowl of temporal stew, she sacrificed the one thing that made her the church.

The marriage of church and state that began with Constantine was a rocky one, with the balance of power fluctuating through the years until finally achieving stasis with the medieval mingling of the temporal and spiritual realms into the rather unsavory concoction of both authorities that was regnant in Luther's day. Virtually any history of Luther or the Reformation era will provide a sufficient number of appalling accounts and examples of the abuses of this dark period of church history to highlight the toxic dangers of cooking the realms into one repugnant stew: bishops commanding armies, popes manipulating princes, and princes buying spiritual legitimacy and even salvation. But, once again, the patently obvious historical example of the failure only serves to alert us to the continuing danger, and the temptation and resultant disaster of collapsing the temporal and spiritual realms into one reality.

Luther ardently denounced the mixture of church and state and delighted in the fact that he had played a significant role in restoring an appropriate distinction between the two realms, empowering secular rulers to shake off the overreach of the church's authority into the secular realm.[3] But the understanding of the church as the ultimate authority in all the world, with all temporal government and every civil ruler in full submission to the church, never fully disappeared. The deeply engrained obsession with papal power and supremacy nurtured the notion that all spiritual and temporal authority should be united under a single ecclesial ruler. H. Richard Niebuhr recognized the strength of the idea in his 1950 classic, *Christ and Culture*. While his discussion of the American version of Roman Catholicism and its necessarily

3 AE 13:42–43.

limited ambitions was carefully and rightly nuanced, his label for the Roman Catholic understanding of the two realms says it all: "Christ over Culture."[4] Even after the attempt to soften some of Rome's hard edges with Vatican II, the idea continues to lurk in the twenty-first century among those labeled or self-described as conservative Roman Catholics. The teaching goes by the name of integralism and holds that the world only works the right way when the church is in charge. Integralists work with varying degrees of transparency and with different approaches but with the common goal of establishing secular governments founded on Christian doctrine and submissive to ecclesial authority.

Positions altogether similar to those of integralism appear with regularity and fervor also among Protestants, especially Evangelicals, who, as Niebuhr would put it, seek to transform the culture.[5] Of course, most Protestants have no interest in a Roman Catholic reign over the world but harbor a keen interest in Christian values and biblical truth gaining supremacy in the halls of American power. In the Protestant world, championing the alignment of secular authority and spiritual authority with the objective of a Christian America is not known as integralism but operates under the label of Christian nationalism. The popularity of Christian nationalism along with the older Roman Catholic integralism seemed to rise with the arrival of pandemic panic in 2020 and following. The reaction against what was interpreted as government overreach and weariness with the steady, society-wide deterioration of traditional mores under the broad label of "woke" ideology emboldened many proponents of nationalist/integralist ideas into a much more public and outspoken posture. The Christian nationalist/Roman integralist solution to the perceived threat from a godless government and a decadent culture was

4 H. Richard Niebuhr, *Christ and Culture* (HarperCollins, 1951), 42, 116–48.
5 Niebuhr, 43, 190–229

to recapture or perhaps conquer the government for the sake of either biblical truth or the church or some combination of the two.

Lutherans seeking to be faithful to their confession and living in the same fraught twenty-first-century American context certainly are not immune to the influence of those seeking to assert Christian truth and triumphalism over secular government and society. Indeed, those who confess the distinction between the two realms in concert with Luther and who rightly seek to hold the government's policies and practices accountable to God's creational law are often intrigued and even lured by the rhetoric and zeal of Christians, whether Catholic or Protestant, who espouse positions consistent with integralism. Some confessional Lutherans may well wonder, "What's not to love about Christian nationalism? What could be better than a government that takes God's truth seriously, that honors the church, and that suppresses what is evil and opposed to the Gospel?"

The answer, of course, is that nothing is wrong with a government operating according to God's truth. As argued above, for Christians, this is precisely the goal. Indeed, a secular ruler who hews to God's Law and cooperates with and supports the church is definitely not at odds with a right understanding of the two realms—no matter how odd such an idea might seem in the present desacralized American context. Faithful Lutherans will no doubt find themselves in sympathy with many, if not most, of the ideas, morals, and objectives of those contending for some form of Christian nationalism. Nevertheless, a right understanding of the two realms coupled with a clear-sighted grasp of the church's purpose will temper their enthusiasm and curb their support for any form of Christian nationalism—even one that claims a Lutheran foundation. The reason goes well beyond a superficial desire to hold the tension between the temporal and spiritual realms out of loyalty to Lutheran ways of operating.

For faithful Lutherans, the much greater problem with Christian nationalism is that it amounts to little more than an exaggerated and enhanced Constantinianism, or perhaps Constantinianism with super powers. Integralism and Christian nationalism both advocate for a form of Christianity that is so consumed with contending for a godly version of temporal justice that it inadvertently neglects and denigrates its commission to proclaim the creation's ultimate justification. Even more alarming is the way that Christian nationalism eviscerates the church's foremost task, indeed her *raison d'être*, of making the Gospel known through the compelling witness of a community of faith founded on the reality of Christ and the way of the cross, and not the way of worldly clout, popular acclaim, public appeal, or political power. The church does not seek earthly control or temporal authority. She does not ever forsake her overriding task to declare God's work in Christ to reclaim and restore the creation. And the church absolutely does not fight to achieve any goal—no matter how holy or noble. Fighting is the way of the sword. The way of the Word is not fighting but earnest proclamation made credible by a winsome witness. Christian nationalism reduces the church to one more special interest group or stakeholder caught up in the machinations and manipulations that define temporal politics. Indeed, by making control of the world their objective, Christian nationalism aims far too low and forfeits her God-given birthright as the harbinger of God's new creation.

THE DEMOCRATIC TEMPTATION

The simplicity of explaining the two realms is too often negated by the apparent difficulty people have in rightly holding the tension. Wrongly dividing the realms can lead to the inaction of quietism and confusing them can result in integralism. Resisting these mistaken ways of operating seems to be even more challenging for

Christians living in the Western world with its deeply embedded love of democratic ideals. As noted above, a democratic republic is arguably one of the least objectionable ways of structuring and exercising governmental authority in the temporal realm. There are good reasons to prefer democracy over monarchies, oligarchies, aristocracies, demagogues, and full-fledged dictatorships. And yet Christians need to bear in mind that democracy is not the biblical way or the Christian way or the God-established way of operating a government. Christian teaching simply doesn't endorse one form of government over another. Difficult as this truth may be to accept, even more challenging is the realization that some of the most foundational and cherished principles that undergird our political commitments are themselves at odds with Christian truth.

The idea that every single human being is born free and endowed with fundamental, inalienable rights inherent in their very being (such as life, liberty, possession of property, and the pursuit of happiness) is axiomatic among Western people, even Christians. And yet that conviction is grounded not in biblical teaching but in Enlightenment ideals of the autonomous individual who is beholden to no man or institution unless willingly chosen for the sake of societal good. It is worth remembering that Christian confession begins not with a self-sufficient, autonomous, capable, rights-wielding individual who consents to have a Lord or chooses a religion worthy of her devotion. Quite the opposite. Christians know that they are from birth helpless, utterly contingent, and wholly dependent. And Christians know their sin; they know their failure. They know that as hopeless sinners, their lives are forfeit, their future is desolate, and because of sin, their eternity is rightfully damnation.

Of course, this bleak, crushing reality is completely transformed in the Gospel of Jesus, who forgives sin, rescues sinners, restores creatures, and brings His creation to its fulfillment in eternal life. Christians know this as well. But when Christians operate according to their Western formation and embrace (usually and understandably without even realizing they are doing it) the foundations and convictions of their fellow citizens of the Enlightened West, they will find themselves contending for ideas, principles, and goals that are at home in individualism, rationalism, and nationalism but out of place in Christian confession. When they step into the temporal realm and especially into the political arena of the world, Christians should consciously and pointedly ask themselves if they are following Jesus into the fray. It is far too easy to follow popular sentiment, nationalistic zeal, or inflated individualistic ideals instead. This is a significant challenge for Christians seeking rightly to maintain a right understanding and practice of the two realms and should be a particular concern for the church's pastors and teachers.

The enduring, undying devotion to democracy so central to Western culture can not only drive Christians to equate their commitment to Christ with a patriotic commitment to their country, but it can often compel them to attempt rather elaborate Christian explanations and defenses for their democratic ideals. This is manifest when Luther's rather unequivocal statements forbidding rebellion or any sort of violent armed insurrection against government are met with efforts to temper, mitigate, or relativize the impact of what is perceived as an unfortunate teaching—unfortunate because it does not comport with democratic convictions about freedom, individual rights, and the will of the people. For a Christian, it should be quite simple: all earthly authority comes from God and God alone. Authority does not come from people or elections or the consent of the governed. Authority comes from God. God gives it. God takes it. So, when Luther affirms these ideas and rebuffs democratic notions, he is not being merely medieval or a lackey of the ruler.[6] Luther, with his teaching about temporal authority and the need for subjects to reject any notion of a right to rebel and to obey their rulers, does not need skillful, enlightened, well-meaning, but slightly embarrassed Lutherans to come to his rescue. Lutherans do not need to rehabilitate Luther and his frankly undemocratic ways of thinking about temporal authority. Instead, they need to see Luther's complete alignment and faithful consistency with the clear teaching of Jesus, Peter, and Paul.

Rejection of cherished Western principles such as individual autonomy, the right of rebellion against wicked and unjust government, or social contract assumptions about the source of authority may not resonate in the twenty-first-century world, but Christians do not conform their doctrine to popular sentiment or rationalist arguments. They adhere to God's revealed truth and the simple admonition to follow Christ's way of self-denial, sacrificial service to neighbor, obedience to rulers, and submission to God's providential care. Yet Christians seeking to follow God's will in the temporal realm may sometimes be perplexed about exactly which authority they are to obey while living in a world marked with civil unrest, populist upheavals, insurrections, coups d'état, revolutions, and foreign occupations. This is a legitimate concern. It is not always obvious which temporal ruler claiming authority actually operates with the divine mandate as "God's servant . . . who carries out God's wrath on the wrongdoer."[7] Whether living in Boston in 1775, Vichy France in 1944, or Donetsk Oblast in 2025, a Christian seeking to be a faithful follower of Christ may well be perplexed about which temporal leader to obey.

The best counsel in times of ambiguity and bewilderment is often simply to wait for clarity to emerge from the fog. But when inaction is impossible or a noncommittal course is unavailable, there are still some principles that can offer guidance. First, in

---

6 AE 45:61–68, 96, 102–3.

7 Romans 13:4.

concert with the concept of subsidiarity that decisions should be made at the lowest possible level of a hierarchy, in times of uncertainty, it is probably advisable to yield to the authority of the nearest, most immediate temporal ruler. Another critical practice is to include the wisdom and counsel of the wider church; in other words, individual Christians should seek to act in unison with the collective discernment of their community—be that a congregation or perhaps, if possible, some even larger grouping of Christians. Finally, even in hazy periods of social and political turmoil, Christians should not be afraid to speak and act with confidence in their Lord, who they know is eager to forgive whatever sins they may inadvertently or unavoidably commit as they seek to follow in the way of Christ. It is also worth noting that in those situations when, after the obscuring mists have at last dissipated, it becomes apparent that God has seen fit to allow the toppling of a dictator through popular revolution, Christians should not persist in refusing to acknowledge the new government, regardless how it came to power, nor should they construe the success of the revolt as divine approval and affirmation of the rebellion.

The challenge of rightly grasping, teaching, and practicing the distinction between the two realms is not easy. But neither is it impossible. It is actually not even overly complicated. Rather, holding a right understanding and practice of the two realms is merely a matter of attending to the clear teaching of both Scripture and Christian confession and of recognizing and renouncing the errant inclinations that arise from within our sinful, self-aggrandizing hearts and from the corrupted, apostate cultures that surround us and seek to form us. Christians who keep a sharp focus on Jesus as their Savior and Lord in all of life will find a sure path through the harsh and often perplexing realities that confront them in a broken world.

Chapter 4
Conclusion

Among Christians, the degree of interest in the Lutheran understanding of the distinction between God's two realms seems to be entirely cyclical. It rises and then ebbs with precise regularity—according to a rather predictable four-year pattern that parallels but has nothing to do with the Olympics. The rise is gradual but increases exponentially toward a sharp spike every fourth November and then the drop-off is immediate and precipitous as people get busy with Thanksgiving plans and the arrival of the Christmas season. No doubt, presidential elections fuel political interest, and it is certainly a very good thing that Christian people make an effort to think rightly—that is, Christianly—about their political lives. This is to say that I fully understand and appreciate the sudden but short-lived fascination with pressing questions and concerns about the two kingdoms or the two realms or church and state that appear every four years. But while I understand the election year fervor and welcome people's interest in thinking rightly about elections, candidates, voting, and the Christian way of living as good citizens, I lament the fact that, for far too many Christians, the distinction between the two realms is little more than a specific, somewhat odd tool to be sought and retrieved from some forgotten corner of theology for a couple weeks of use every four years. The teaching of the two realms is so much more.

It needs to be stressed with fervor and frequency that the two realms teaching is not a synonym for issues of church and state. There is considerably more involved with a right grasp of God's work in each of the two realms than merely questions about the proper interface between ecclesiastical and governmental agendas and affairs. Any discussion about the realms that starts and stops with church and state is woefully inadequate and does not serve God's people well. It is critical, then, to begin with, and then maintain, a wide and robust grasp of the significance and scope of the two realms. All of life fits within this distinction. Indeed, there is not a single part of any individual's life that does not map directly to one of the two realms: one is either centering effort and attention on the relationships and reality of the material world, or it is the spiritual, God-ward relationship that is in focus. The right-hand, spiritual realm encompasses the latter, and the left-hand, temporal realm is concerned with the former.

Every human without exception lives always and only within the compass of both realms, which map precisely with the two kinds of righteousness. Those without faith and so without true righteousness before God nonetheless live as creatures before God whether they acknowledge Him or not. They encounter His reality as a nagging awareness of something missing or as a mystery that confounds their ability to understand or as a menacing threat to their very existence that they try to flee. In the spiritual realm, God's Law confronts and convicts every creature. Even those who shun and deny God are aware of Him and will often attempt to replace Him with other "spiritual" components intended to fill the void or blunt the conviction they encounter in the spiritual realm. The spiritual realm reality of Christians also begins with the accusing Law that exposes life's futility and nurtures despair. But having heard and received the gift of rescue and reconciliation given through the life, death, and resurrection of Jesus, Christians have righteousness before God. They are able to delight in their relationship with the Creator and Lord of the world and confidently anticipate the coming full and complete re-creation of God's good world. For Christian believers, the spiritual realm is flooded with the Gospel.

While unbelievers may dispute the reality or importance of the spiritual realm, few of them reject the significant reality of the temporal, material realm that encompasses them. The truth, of course, is that both unbelievers living apart from God's grace and believers who receive and revel in that grace always live fully within the temporal, left-hand realm. The problem, though, is that Christians are prone—perhaps in reaction against the "worldliness" of unbelievers or, more likely, merely because of long habit and lingering, spiritualizing ideas—to minimize, trivialize, or even spurn their temporal realm lives, joys, and responsibilities. Christians need to be reminded that while they are fully spiritual creatures, they are also fully material creatures who live immersed in a material world.

The materiality of Christians' lives is not a burden they should lament, nor is it a menacing temptation they must reject. The materiality of their lives is a truth they should embrace and celebrate as an essential component of their humanity. Thus, Christians marry and raise children and pursue hobbies and sports; they enjoy food and fellowship with others and celebrate the stunning and wildly varying wonder and beauty of the creation all around them; they strive to understand the intricacies and mysteries of the material world for the sheer delight, and the implicit worship, of thinking God's thoughts after Him. The material realm is not in opposition to the spiritual—it is its perfect complement. The material realm is the arena for which humans were created and the place where they fulfill God's will for their lives. There is nothing inherently ugly, evil, or anti-spiritual about the material world that God created and continues to preserve. Christians need to be encouraged to embrace the reality, goodness, and holiness of the temporal realm.

Recognizing our essential human materiality helps us more highly to regard the significance and sacredness of the work we are given to do in the world. Luther's other breakthrough, his realization of the centrality of our vocations grounded in family and community relationships, is perhaps the most important aspect of the teaching of the two realms. It far surpasses even the teaching's significance in guiding Christians rightly to understand church and state relations. Learning to see how good and holy it is that our lives are tied intricately and absolutely to the tangible, physical, earthly, material reality that defines us is a sine qua non for humans to live meaningful, purposeful, joyful, and God-pleasing lives. Clearly, this truth matters every day through every season of an entire human life. The two realms teaching is not an every four years novelty like periodical cicadas. It is a foundational truth at the heart of Christian confession that enables and then empowers human creatures to live their lives aligned with God's intention. The two realms teaching delivers both the spiritual realm Gospel and grace that makes humans whole and joyful along with the temporal realm Law and guidance that makes them purposeful and fulfilled. We cannot operate rightly as human creatures without a proper grasp of the two realms.

A robust teaching and understanding of the two realms also reinforces and extends the dynamic interaction between the passive contemplation and celebration of God and His gifts on the one hand and the active service and achievements for the sake of fellow creatures on the other. This twofold reality lies at the core of a rightly ordered human life.[1] God designed us to live in communion with Him and with other creatures, to receive what He freely delivers, and then in turn to pour ourselves out in service to others. This is what it means to be human. And this is what it means to champion a Lutheran ethic that is occupied not with self-improvement, the pursuit of individual morality, or attaining

---

1 This interface between the realms as a critical key in understanding the scriptural narrative as well as our lives within God's story is explored more fully in my book *Day 7: For Work, Rest, or Play* (Concordia Publishing House, 2024).

loftier degrees of personal rectitude but instead centers on selfless service to others and on dying to self for the sake of living for Christ and the neighbor. The two realms foundation makes clear the normative and all-encompassing orientation of our lives that is rightly fixed on service to those around us.

Finally, the two realms teaching also maps seamlessly to the two great commissions of the biblical narrative. The left-hand realm's focus on the temporal reality is confirmed in God's first great commission delivered in Genesis: "Be fruitful and multiply and fill the earth and subdue it, and have dominion over the fish of the sea and over the birds of the heavens and over every living thing that moves on the earth."[2] And the right-hand realm's singular emphasis on the spiritual reality between Creator and creature is the concern of the New Testament commission to proclaim the Gospel as articulated by Jesus: "Go therefore and make disciples of all nations, baptizing them in the name of the Father and of the Son and of the Holy Spirit, teaching them to observe all that I have commanded you."[3] Christians live their lives in light of both commissions. When they are fulfilling the first commission, they secure opportunity and credibility for the work of the second commission. Believers will be intent on obeying both divine commissions. They live to serve the temporal, material needs of other creatures and they live to meet the eternal, spiritual needs of those same creatures. In other words, followers of Christ purposefully work to bring God's world more fully into conformity with God's intent. Christians do that work most rightly and effectively by serving their neighbors, no doubt; but even more importantly, they do that work by telling God's Gospel story about Jesus to those around them, inviting those creatures also to delight in God's grace and to join them as part of God's people, His community of faith. The

---

2 Genesis 1:28.

3 Matthew 28:19–20.

church must never lose sight of her singular and defining *raison d'être* to make known the Gospel of free forgiveness, new life, and eternal hope in Jesus Christ.

The teaching of the two realms is not a Lutheran oddity, a fraught paradox, an unresolvable feud, or even a precarious tension that exhausts those who seek to maintain its delicate balance. The teaching of the two realms is simply a faithful expression of God's merciful provision for His creation. Even in its fallen state, God continues to care for His world through the two realms. Creatures who recognize this twofold plan and live in accord with it not only thrive, but they live in joyful delight as God intended. Of course, sin and the selfishness, separation, sorrow, and suffering that always follow in its wake pollutes and spoils the operation of both realms. That sad reality will continue to cast its cold, dark, and painful shadow until the day that Christ fulfills His promise and returns in glory to His creation. On that day of resurrection and new creation, sin's destructive power and reign will be crushed forever. And on that day, the two realms will be swept up together into God's grand, eternal plan for His creation. They will be fully reconciled, fully reunited, and fully realized in the perfect fullness of Christ.